Preview Page

Two Layer _____ Cake

Drink A Tall Glass Of _____

Corn On The _____

_____ On The Grill

Connecting Edible Memories

Book 1 of 3

This Coloring Book Is Designed With Simple Familiar Black-Line Drawings
With Sentence Cuing Common Phrases For Cognitive Art Therapy - For All Ages .
Recommended At Home One On One, With A Caregiver Or Family Member
And As A Resource For Therapeutic Recreation Departments.

35 Single Sided Coloring Pages, Plus
20 Keepsake Home-Cooking Recipe Inspired Journal Pages

———————

The Adult Coloring Book Craze Is Here.

*Bonnie has created a great activities resource that can be used individually
on a one on one basis or in a group setting. It's simple familiar designs,
color-cuing and common phrases allow for successful completion.
Providing a positive, calm and fun experience.
I highly recommend it's use with anyone with cognitive impairment.
Every therapeutic recreation department should utilize this amazing
resource as they will immediately see the denefits.
Recommended By; Alexis Chiucarello, Director Of Therapeutic Recreation
And Dementia Program Coordinator Long Term Center.*

———————

Illustrator and Author: Bonnie S. MacLachlan

Publisher: Art.Z illustrations
Griswold, Ct
ArtZillustrations.com

Special Thanks To: Alexis Chiucarello

Made In America
Copyright 2016 © Bonnie S. MacLachlan

Art.Z illustrations
ISBN-13: 978-09977889-5-2
ISBN-10: 099778895X

Author - Illustrator retains 100% of all design concepts and copyrights.
No part of this book or idea may be recreated for sale, reproduced or
transmitted electronic or mechanical, including photocopying, scanning and
recording or by information storage and retrievable system.

All Rights Reserved

_____ On The Grill

Juicy Hamburger On A _____ With _____

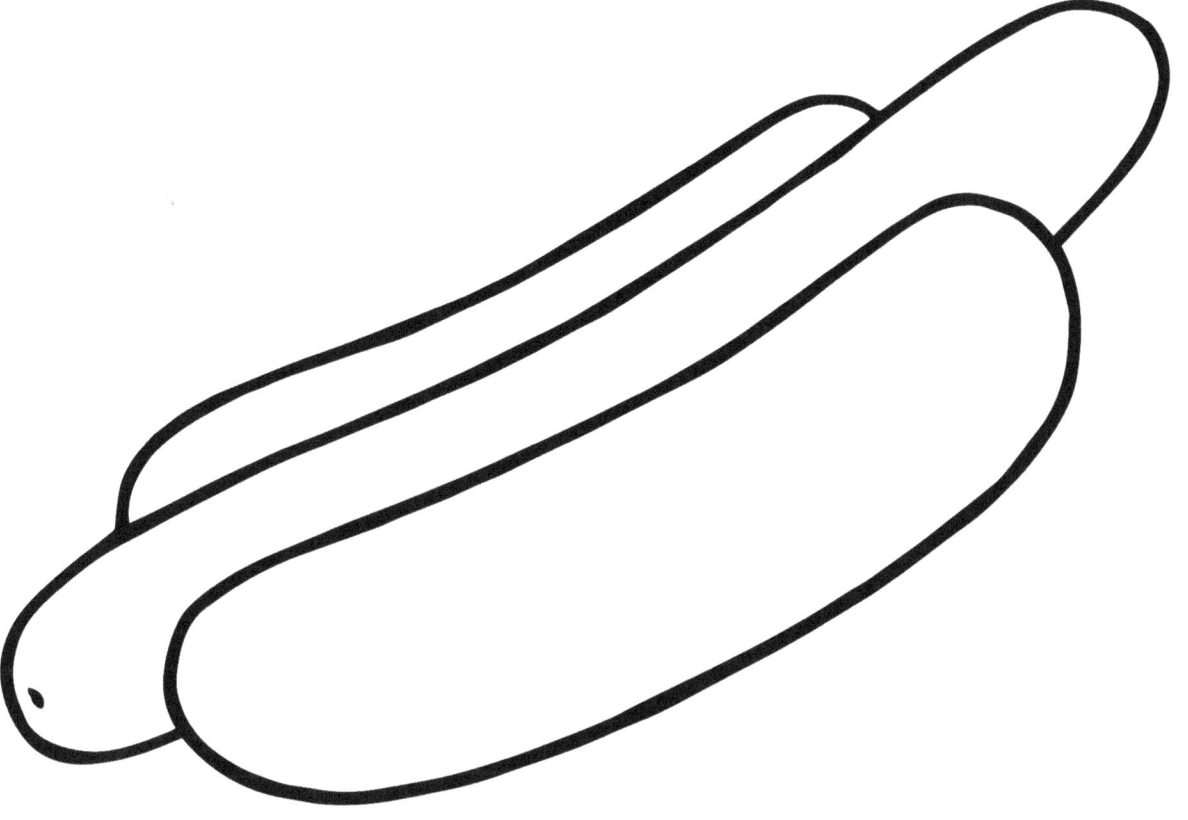

Hotdog, Ketchup And _____

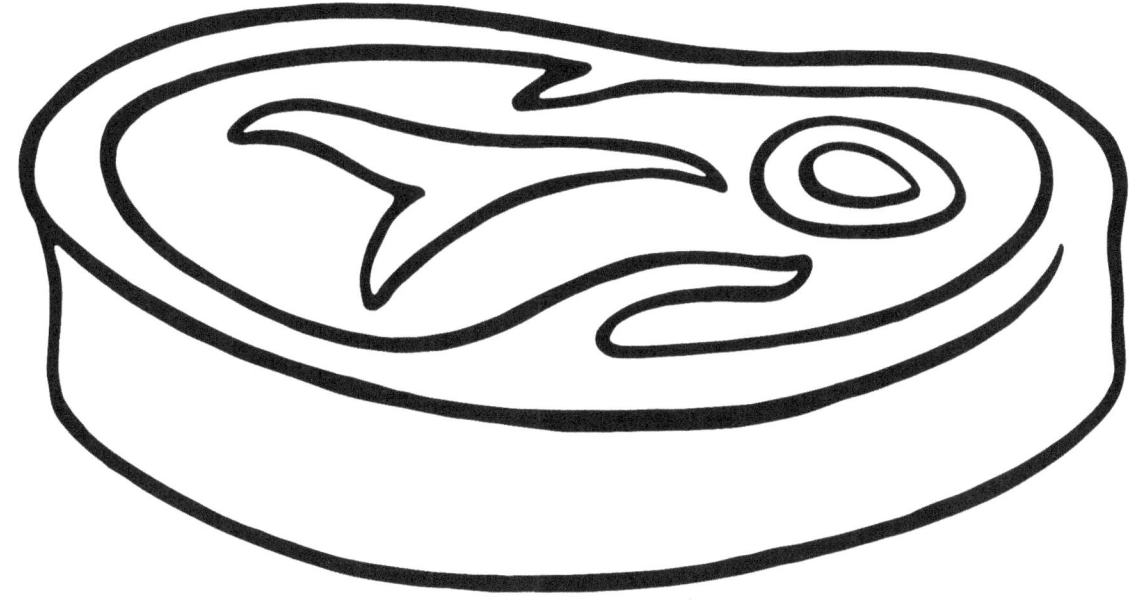

_____ Steak With _____

_____ And _____ Sandwich

Ketchup And _____

_____ Mustard

Salt And _____

I Eat _____
With A _____

Drink A Tall Glass Of _____

Glass Of _____ Beer

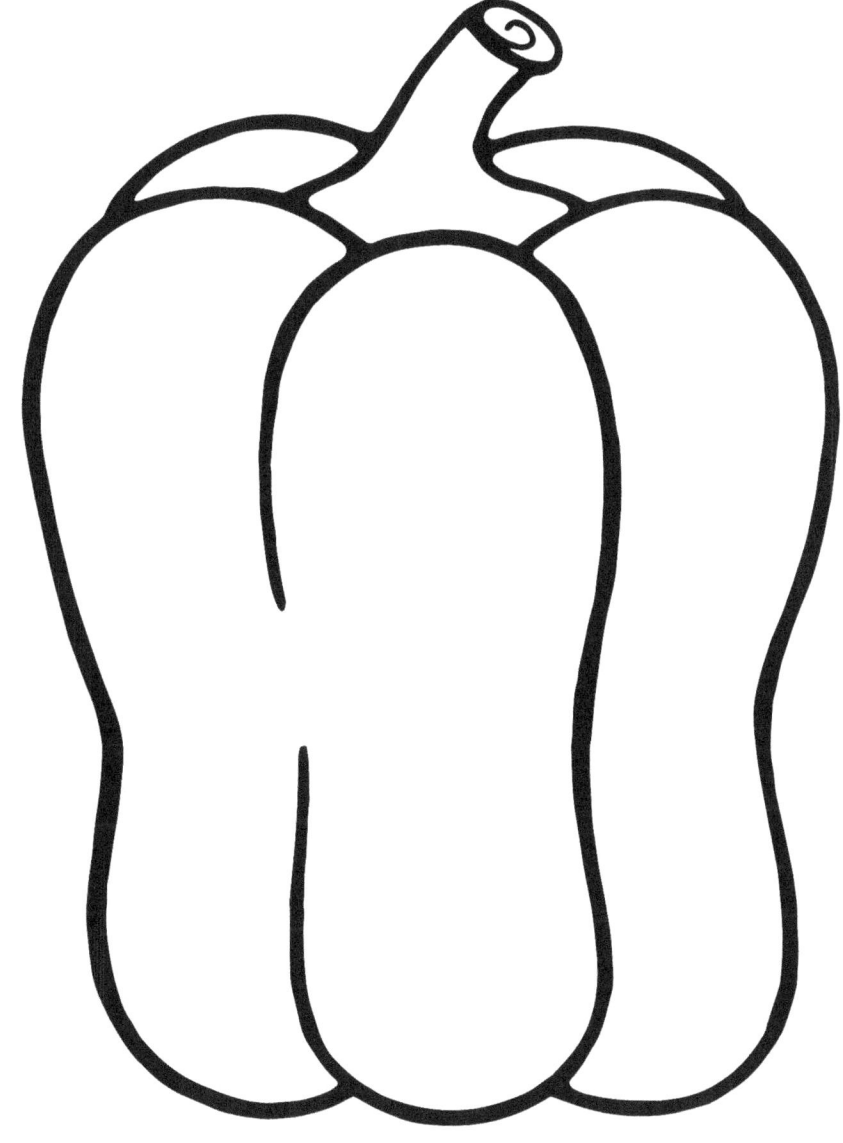

Fried Peppers And _____

_____ Potatoes And _____

Corn On The _____

Eggplant _____

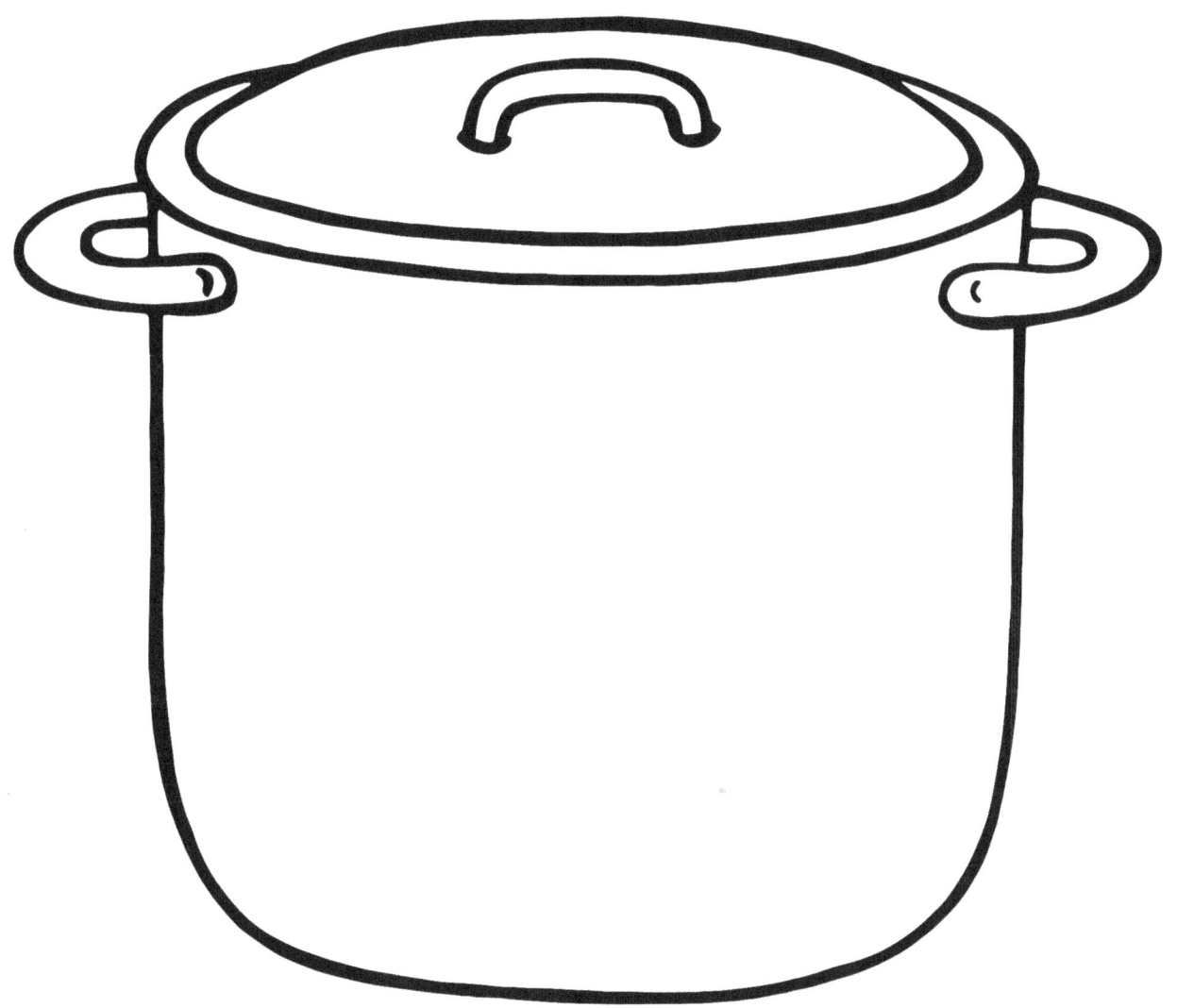

_____ Pot

Crabs _____

_____ Milk

Peanut Butter And
_____ Sandwich

Bananas And _____

Juicy _____ Pear

Cherry _____

Pineapple _____

A Big _____
Of _____ Grapes

Strawberries And _____

The Fridge Is Filled With _____

I Love Cooking _____

_____ Apron

Mixing _____ Cookie Dough

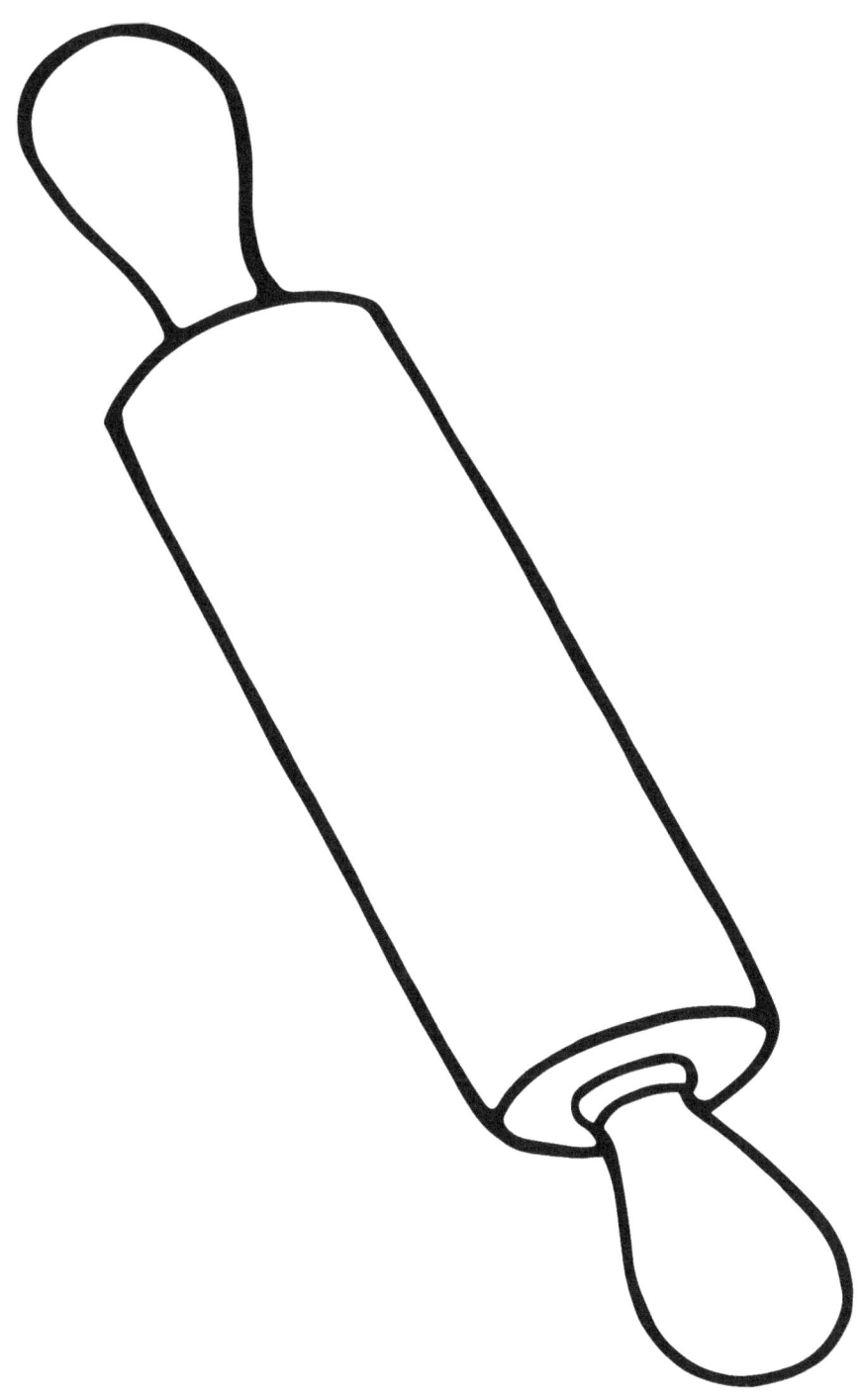

Yummy _____ Dough

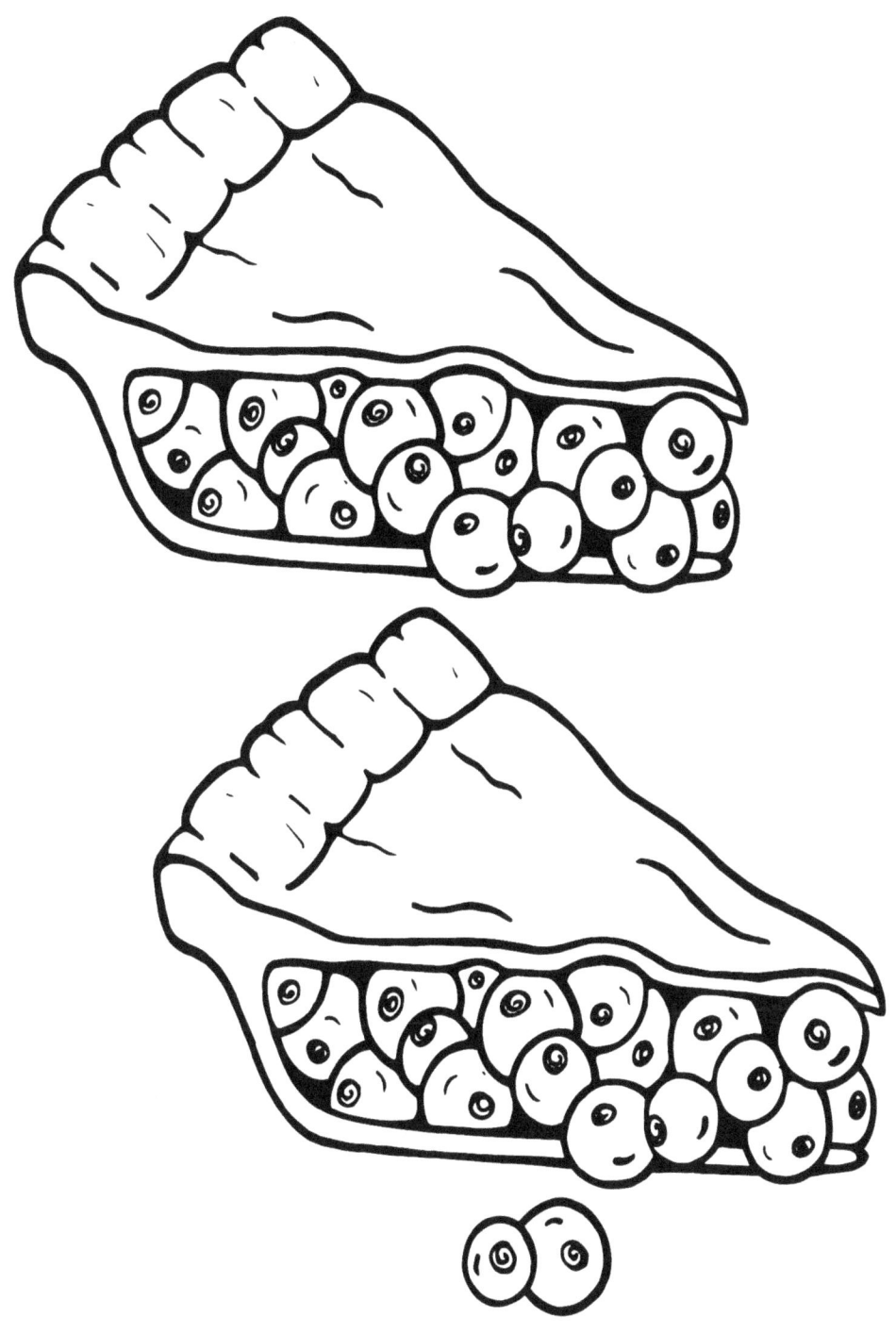

_____ Pieces

Of _____ Pie

Two Layer _____ Cake

_____ Ice Cream
In A _____ Cone

_____ Flavored Lolly Pop

20 Keepsake Home-Cooking Recipe Inspired Journal Pages

As you go through the pages of this book, memories of all kinds of food recipes and loving, fun, sweet stories with family and friends, will inevitably be remembered.

Use the following pages to keep record of these precious memories, to prevent them from being lost forever.

Edible Stories

Who
Where
When

Connecting Edible Memories

Recipe _____

Ingredients: _____
_____
_____
_____
_____
_____
_____
_____
_____

Directions: _____
_____
_____
_____
_____
_____
_____
_____
_____
_____
_____
_____
_____

Connecting Edible Memories

Edible Stories

Who
Where
When

Connecting Edible Memories

Recipe _____

Ingredients: _____
_____
_____
_____
_____
_____
_____
_____
_____

Directions: _____
_____
_____
_____
_____
_____
_____
_____
_____
_____
_____
_____
_____

Connecting Edible Memories

Edible Stories

Who
Where
When

Connecting Edible Memories

Recipe _____

Ingredients:
_____
_____
_____
_____
_____
_____
_____
_____
_____

Directions:
_____
_____
_____
_____
_____
_____
_____
_____
_____
_____
_____
_____
_____

Connecting Edible Memories

Edible Stories

Who
Where
When

Connecting Edible Memories

Recipe _____

Ingredients:
_____
_____
_____
_____
_____
_____
_____
_____
_____

Directions:
_____
_____
_____
_____
_____
_____
_____
_____
_____
_____
_____

Connecting Edible Memories

Edible Stories

**Who
Where
When**

Connecting Edible Memories

Recipe _____

Ingredients:

Directions:

Connecting Edible Memories

Edible Stories

Who
Where
When

Connecting Edible Memories

Recipe _____

Ingredients:
_____
_____
_____
_____
_____
_____
_____
_____

Directions:
_____
_____
_____
_____
_____
_____
_____
_____
_____
_____
_____
_____

Connecting Edible Memories

Edible Stories

Who
Where
When

Connecting Edible Memories

Recipe _____

Ingredients:
_____
_____
_____
_____
_____
_____
_____
_____
_____

Directions:
_____
_____
_____
_____
_____
_____
_____
_____
_____
_____
_____
_____
_____

Connecting Edible Memories

Edible Stories

Who
Where
When

Connecting Edible Memories

Recipe _____

Ingredients: _____
_____
_____
_____
_____
_____
_____
_____
_____

Directions: _____
_____
_____
_____
_____
_____
_____
_____
_____
_____
_____
_____
_____

Connecting Edible Memories

Edible Stories

Who
Where
When

Connecting Edible Memories

Recipe _____

Ingredients:
_____
_____
_____
_____
_____
_____
_____
_____
_____

Directions:
_____
_____
_____
_____
_____
_____
_____
_____
_____
_____
_____
_____
_____

Connecting Edible Memories

Edible Stories

Who
Where
When

_____
_____
_____
_____
_____
_____
_____
_____
_____
_____
_____
_____
_____
_____
_____
_____
_____
_____
_____
_____
_____
_____

Connecting Edible Memories

Recipe _____

Ingredients:
_____
_____
_____
_____
_____
_____
_____
_____

Directions:
_____
_____
_____
_____
_____
_____
_____
_____
_____
_____
_____

Connecting Edible Memories

Go To ArtZillustrations.com For More
Interactive Coloring Books, Adult Coloring Books, Journals & Products

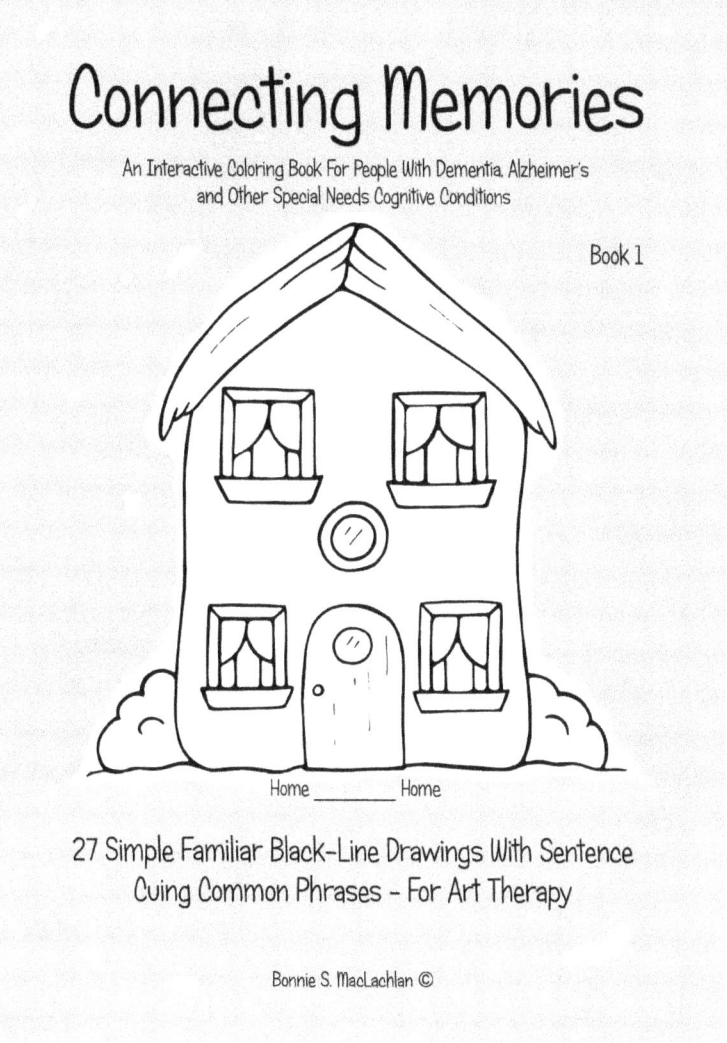

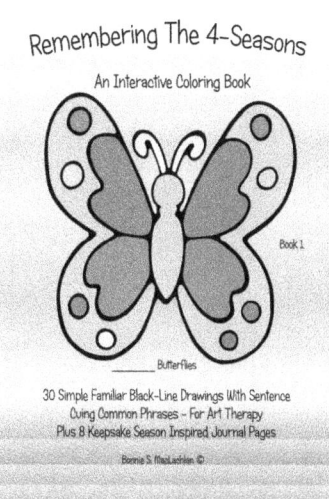

Bonnie S. MacLachlan ©   www.ArtZillustrations.com

www.ingramcontent.com/pod-product-compliance
Lightning Source LLC
Chambersburg PA
CBHW081017040426
42444CB00014B/3245